Deception and Consequences Revealed

Deception and Consequences Revealed

You Shall Know the Truth and the Truth Shall Set You Free

Bill Vincent

Deception and Consequences Revealed
Copyright © 2014 by Bill Vincent. All rights reserved.

No part of this publication may be reproduced, stored in a retrieval system or transmitted in any way by any means, electronic, mechanical, photocopy, recording or otherwise without the prior permission of the author except as provided by USA copyright law.

Published By
Revival Waves of Glory Books & Publishing
PO Box 596
Litchfield, IL 62056

Revival Waves of Glory Books & Publishing is committed to excellence in the publishing industry.

Published in the United States of America

eBook: 978-1-312-58396-2
Paperback: 978-0692534663
Hardcover: 978-1-312-58395-5

REL012120 RELIGION / Christian Life / Spiritual Growth
REL108010 RELIGION / Christian Church / Growth
REL012070 RELIGION / Christian Life / Personal Growth

Table of Contents

Introduction 7
Chapter 1 Book Trilogies 11
    Divergent 13
    Matched 15
    Hunger Games 16
    The Book of Life 17
Chapter 2 Phone Apps 19
    The Vine and Instagram 19
Chapter 3 Scamming Christians 25
    Jim and Lori Bakker 26
    The Harbinger 29
    Covertness False Prophets 30
Chapter 4 False Teachings 33
    Joel and Victoria Osteen 35
    Oprah Winfrey 42
    Joseph Prince 44
About the Author 57
Recommended Books 59

Introduction

I thank you Lord. When you release warnings, we are going to listen and honor at your word that your warnings are for a reason. Lord, you said release a warning of a sneak attack. That's exactly what the enemy is trying to do, is sneak right into the body of the Christ in a way to cause salvation not to be average in the church and to cause children to become more rebelling and rebellious than ever before. Thank you Lord Jesus.

First of all, I want you to understand that we have gone through much of this in our own home before I even preach it. God gave me a title and he said "Warning of a sneak attack." When I say sneak attack, I'm not talking about 9/11. I'm not talking about somebody crashing into a side of a building with a plane. I'm not talking about any terrorism. What I'm talking about is the enemy infiltrating the body of Christ, and infiltrating the school just so subtle that we are accepting it as common law. We are accepting the changes that are going on in this world and we need to stop.

We're not in China. We're not in Russia. We are in the United States of America that was founded on God, in God, and we should stay in God. Hallelujah. I want you to understand that our nation is in dire need. Our children are more rebellious than I've ever seen in my life. I thought I was rebellious, but my goodness, I didn't even know the word rebellion. I want you to understand that I have seen in the spirit for a long time and God has given me identity to some of the strategies, some of the tools that the enemy is using that some of us don't see because we receive it because our schools are pushing it, and things are happening in this direction.

God has been speaking for a while, but I want you to know what the enemy is using for sneak attacks, he is using things for sneak attacks and every few months, God begins to lay things in my heart completely, to put God's finger on it. This is more like a Watchman of the Lord and I want you to understand that every time God releases these things, it's very powerful and it's for such a time as this. I believe this is probably going to be the most critical of all.

This is the most serious time to protect our children before the enemy pulls them down. The most serious time and some of you should relate to, what's been going on in this region. Some of the things that's going on, I'm telling you, let me go ahead and say. It's not about races. It's not about anything that's going on in this country. What's going on in this country is there's a demon from hell that is pulling children and is trying to take them for his own. I'm telling you some of us don't realize and we think all children are protected. They're just fine, they're safe.

Let me go ahead and say. I know that I know that I know there's more sexual relations going on between children at 12, 13 years old than you would ever think. Don't think your child is always safe just because you think so. I'm not here to build a fan club. I want you to know that Satan is using, television, Hollywood, even authors of books to pull us down... They're being used by Satan to pull children into rebellion. Apps, downloadable on any phone, are being used to pull the children and distract them.

Chapter 1
Book Trilogies

I want you to understand and I want you to hear this. There's a release of rebellion, sex, mild romance that leads to sexual relations, role-playing and violence. Let me go ahead and say. Most things that are being written right now are coming out in trilogies. There's a reason why because they're not just writing one they're writing several books with the same theme to pull children in.

The teachers are pushing these books. The reason why is because they're number 1 bestsellers already, they're New York Times bestseller. Let me go ahead and say. If I can take all the books that I'm going to talk about and I can take lines out of every book and write to the next book because it just keeps repeating the same cycle over and over, and over again. There is rebellion, sex, violence, destruction. It's aimed towards children.

I want you to understand that I have seen first hand where someone will read this type of book and they will turn the way they respond to their parent. You say, "Oh, I don't believe this can happen." Let me go ahead and say. Do you believe the Word of God? When you read the Word of God, you can be changed. Let me go ahead and say. There are writings being written that are not from the word of God. They're not from God at all. When you read them, you are changed but it's not for the good. It's for evil.

I had a family member that used to read books that were romance novels. You know the type of romance novels. Usually in the 99 cent aisle. They have the couple half-dressed people on the cover and you read them. You either blush or sweat, whichever one you got. I'm telling you this girl became so intertwined with sex and perversion. She became a homosexual by age 13.

I know that I know that I know one day I looked at her dead in the eye and I said I know that these books are your source. I took them all off her bookshelf and I burned them, and I commanded the demon to come out. That girl was set free of that homosexuality right there in front of me.

I want you to understand. I want you to understand that that is something that some people will never believe, that books can turn you that way. Let me go ahead and say. That's exactly what this world is moving toward. If you look at television, there's somebody that's gay on the television. If you got a show that you like, there's always got to be a gay person on it now. You say why? Because this is a nation that accepted homosexuality. The church has accepted. I'm going to really get into that later. The church is accepting homosexuality as a common theme and there's even preachers on television that are saying homosexual will go to heaven without saying, "God, forgive me."

Let me go ahead and say. That's a lie from the pit of hell. It's an abomination and I'm telling you God loves them, but they're going to have to repent. Some are using symbols and respect the demonic strongholds like the sun, and using the sun for the sun God. The devil worship pentagram are being intermixed with the symbols on these books. There's also witchcraft associated symbols of control that are being put in these books. I want you to understand that just because a symbol is not identical doesn't mean that it's not being portrayed to be something different.

Let me go ahead and tell you. The reason why is because if they put a pentagram on every book, it would be something that none of us would be able to understand. We would never receive it. We would never let our child read it. If they just put a circle or swirl on the front cover, a lot of us will look at it and say, oh, well, that must just be fire. That must be just this. That must be just that.

Divergent

That's the way the devil works. Somebody is getting nervous. Understand I am extremely careful when it comes to dropping names. The fear of the Lord is all over me as I was even seeking the Lord about all that I'm going through right now. I can't remember any time that I've mentioned a person by name over the last many years, but the first thing I want to talk about is several books. One that God laid on my heart and I have jerked it out of anybody's hand in my own home. It's called Divergent. It's trilogy. Some of you will say, oh, that's a mild book, but I'm telling you there's competition in the book that is … It all starts minor.

They all started the minor play. They all have started at minor roles. You say why, because they're trying to pull you in. I haven't read all these books. I'm discerning these books. I don't like every book that a child brings into my home. I don't like every one of them. I probably don't like many of them but that's beside the point. There's some that I say no to because of the discerning of spirits. I have nothing against an author that writes a book, but what I do have is against something that is trying to lead our children astray.

In this book, they had been warned in it that can even mean death. Children should not be reading anything about death. There is something about these books that are focused on 12 - 17-year-olds. I don't know about you but my child should not be looking and reading about death unless they're reading about Jesus.

There's also mentioned about a perfect society. Let me go ahead and say. That's part of the end times. It's where they're getting into. When the anti-Christ rises up, a lot of people that take the mark of the beast are going to assume they're in a perfect society where the world has had finally a savior that is really tipping over our world. Guess what? That's a false facade.

Let me say this. This book is so associated with love and sexual perverse things, and it's drawing fantasy out of our children. I'm telling you. You can have an innocent 11-year-old to read that book, and all of a sudden she has a desire when she looks at a boy that she didn't have before. Now, I'm telling you that is exactly what the enemy is doing. I wouldn't say this unless God said it.

Matched

Another book, like I said, these books are fitting together. It could be written by the same person, so to speak. I know they're not but they could be. Another series is called the Matched trilogy. Another book that is very popular, being pushed by our schools again. It's another society. Again, it's that word society. Officials decide whom you love, where you work, when you die. This is books portrayed for children. Our children are reading these books. Teachers are encouraging. Why? Because, again, they're number 1 bestsellers and they're encouraged to be part of reading not just the one book but all the books.

Let me say something. They have to make a choice between perfection which is the society or passion. I don't know about you but any 12-year-old boy or girl should not have any passion in them when it comes to sexual relations of any kind. There should be no looking at another boy or girl. What happened to courtship? Come on. I looked at one book cover in the spirit. I asked somebody. I said, "When do they kiss?" I knew that there was kissing that took place in that book. The reason why is because it seems simple. It seems subtle. If you look all over the Internet, all the Christian organizations will say it's mild.

Yeah. There's the thing called soft porn too. That's not mild enough for my children. Do you hear what I say? Mild? Come on.

This book, again, intertwines with another one. Here's the thing. In that book, they have a love triangle and that's the thing too. Our children should not … Let me go ahead and say. The bible says there is one man. You have a man in your future that you're supposed to have. You're supposed to have one. That's what the bible indicates.

Now, some of us had made bad choices but we're not going to go there, but God made one choice. Your body belongs to your husband is what the bible says. It doesn't say all the husbands you will have.

Hunger Games

Another book, this is probably not going to hit as good as those, that fits, again, intertwine with the first 2 books, is Hunger Games. That book got a lot stronger. You say why. This book was spoken to me as soon as I heard about it.

Again, it's about Capitol district. It's about some kind of organization, another society. I'm telling you. These all fit hand in hand and I know many of you are either reading or have read it, watched the movies, loved them. Let's move on.

It's districts forcing them to live a certain way. Its children are being forced to kill and survive. I'm telling you. That's, again, nothing our children should be focusing on. Children are buying bow and arrows because of this movie. They're figuring out violence because of a movie. You say, oh, it's mild. Let's go ahead and step in just a little deeper. These are between the ages of 12 and 18 who participate in the annual game called Hunger Games and they fight to death on live TV. That should not be done in a Christian home.

In other words, it's a death sentence. Some child has to die. Somebody is going to die. It's a death sentence. You win or you lose. You say, oh, that's just mild. That's not that bad. There's people out there saying, "I see God in it." Raise up a way a child should go and they will not depart from it. That's exactly right. Here's another one I'm just stepping over these pretty quick. The reason why is because when God tells me something is wrong with something, I don't really need to stand on it for a while.

The Book of Life

When God speaks, I believe and I receive. I say, hey, man. I'm out. Thank you Lord. This is what God said to talk about. It's called The Book of Life. That's one of the names of the Bible. One of the names that people call the Bible is the book of life.

The author has written books called Shadow of Night, but this Book of Life is the book that I'm talking about. The subtitle is All Souls Trilogy. It's trying to claim all the souls. Again, it's a series of books. Another book that she went through is ... She wrote about had a vampire scientist in it. You don't need a whole lot of revelation on this. It has a discovery of witchcraft and witches, the discovery that watches or witches in Shadows of the Night. This is the book of life she writes. Do you know why? Because she's trying to step out of her demonic books and step into the teenage realm. People, don't look into books. They don't study a person.

We get busy as parents. We do. We're busy doing something. Our child likes to walk up with an app flashing. I need your password. We're like, yeah, yeah, whatever. What is it? Sometimes it made you to stop, look and listen. Too many parents have allowed children to have Facebook accounts. There's actually a rule that they're not supposed to have it until a certain age. We break the rules on behalf of our children. Why are we teaching that? What do we teach them?

Chapter 2

Phone Apps

I'm not going to apologize for what I'm saying. The reason why is because if it says a certain age, there's a reason why. I'm going to talk about an app later that when it was created the minimum age was 12. After all the pornography was released on it, now the minimum age is 17.

The Vine and Instagram

You say why. Most children are on it and it's called the Vine. I'm going to get on it later. Some people say it's only about who you follow. If you follow and they follow and this person and this person, and they request you ... I was on somebody's phone not too long ago and I looked on Instagram. All I did was look at some friend's story and a nude girl popped up. This is on a young girl's phone, 100% nude.

Then I Googled that girl on the Internet and her picture's on Google from the Instagram, they post your picture on Instagram. Your child is getting put on the web and it will never ever be able to come down, because they have a license that they accepted just by signing up. You know what that means? In my home, Instagram is fired. You say, oh, we should not control children so much. No. There's a thing we say yes to and a thing we say no to.

I knew some families that use to allow children to drink beer, and guess what? They became alcoholics. Raise up the way a child should go. I'm not here to make friends. This is not about to get popular. This is not going to cause my status to be raised. I'm not going to be trending on Twitter tonight because of this. I already know. Thank you Lord. Come on.

This is serious business. You don't think the devil is going to come and say, "Hey, I'm going to use this stuff to cause the eye gates and ear gates of the children to be persuaded this way and rebellions enter in." Devil doesn't announce.

Has the devil ever said this," I'm going to mess you up?" He doesn't say, "Hey, I'm about to get to all the children in the United States through this little app. It's going to be a little Facebook and I'm just going to cause them to accept." God told me to say something later and I'm saying it now because I might not be able to say it later, is nothing is really private.

These things say privacy, it's not really because your friend can share your photo, and some of those photos that you can take that has a timer on them. I know that there are young girls that are taking up images of their body with these timer photos, that once you watch them and the timer goes out you can't open them again. The thing is people are taking stills of them, which means they take a couple clicks on their phone and it actually takes a picture. They repost that all over the place.

You're like, oh, I thought it was private. I thought they couldn't do that. I'm staying here because God didn't let me leave. I know some children that are being not ... They're not allowed to use some of these apps. They're actually downloading the app, using it. Then after they use it they delete so nobody sees it.

Some of us think our children are not real savvy, not real cunning. Let me go ahead and say, I was pretty good when I was a kid.

The thing is I used to get mad when my mom would search my room. You know what? As long as you live in my house, I say it's open. Sometimes you have to look. Sometimes you have to look around and you should have a legal right to look around. It's not invading privacy. It's something that a parent should do because they love their child. Computers should not be locked in the bedroom.

The next one is Instagram. I told you already that Instagram is an app that people can download. Mostly children download it to take pictures and to share much like Facebook. It says literally on Instagram you must be 13 years old to have Instagram. Like I said, all I did was ... I was on somebody's profile and I was looking at something and immediately a naked picture of a girl popped up on a 12, or 11 year old girl's phone. She is private, but this was a friend's friend. It wasn't her. It was a friend's friend. That's why I say nothing's private.

Let me say as far as I'm concerned that thing is never going to be in our house because it is something that can corrupt a child. We're not going to protect her from everything but guess what, I've got to take a stand where we could take a stand.

The next one is 10,000 times worse and that's the Vine. It's actually called Vine. Vine. It's actually flooded images of pornography on it so much so that it was a 12 year old was the rule and it's gotten to be 17 now you have to be to be able to download it.

You can actually set your children's phones. You might have to talk to your company but you can set your children's phones to put their age or birth date in it to where they can't download something if you actually set it that way. As far as I'm concerned I would set your child's phone. If they're not that age, I would set it about 5 years back. You say why? Because they shouldn't have that anyway. If it's got pornography you say, "Oh, again?" They say it's a friend's friend. I'm going to go ahead and say again, it doesn't matter. That is nothing but a way to just cop out of the whole thing.

It's got plenty of inappropriate content that is inappropriate for children. Makes fun of people with mental disabilities, it makes fun of people exposing them. It's actually gotten people so corrupt. There was a teacher in our own school there in Litchfield that actually ... A student took a picture of her, drew a picture of a man's certain appendage in her mouth and sent it to all these places around the school.

As far as I'm concerned that one act should take all phones out of school. That one act should stop any child from having a phone in school. It really should. I believe that. I know some of our own family wouldn't like that but hey, one child blows it for everybody. They're supposed to be going to school to get taught, not out to text and chat and take pictures and do other stuff. I don't know about you but they're on that enough.

There's really no such thing as private. One thing God is really wanting to put his finger on to is clothes that are shrinking. Put your clothes on. Guess what? There's no booty shorts in heaven. Hallelujah. They print stuff on the back of people's shorts now. In their short shorts enough I don't need to have to read while I look. Even if you're right and you're pure those letters draw your eyes. That's what that's for.

I'm telling you, low cut tops is really minor compared to the short shorts today and the short miniskirts and all different things. I'm telling you and they're wearing it to schools. I'm telling you, we need to start taking a stand and say, "If the school is not going to take a stand for it we need to take a stand when we send our children to school."

Underwear has become out of wear. I know I probably don't have time for this last one but here's the thing. Teaching is going on in our school all across the nation teaching about science, evolution, but not Christian beliefs. They're teaching about that we came from monkeys or frogs or some Big Bang Theory but they're not teaching anything about Jesus and Adam and Eve. They will actually teach about civil rights and about homosexuality but they're not even talking about Adam and Even.

Chapter 3
Scamming Christians

Another thing that is going on across our nation is scamming Christians. Christians are falling to scams all over America and it's demonic. It's not God. Christians are innocent easy prey. These scams are oriented to say, "It's time for the church to be blessed. We are a Christian organization trying to help you." Most of them are pyramid schemes. Most of them are some kind of products and you'll make some money. Well, guess what? Most of them are false. Most of them are lies from the pit of hell and most of them are out to get your money.

If you make any money from it, you just happen to be one of the blessed ones. Most of them are there to take your money. This is really becoming so corrupt that when somebody has a good idea in the future it's really from God because I know some people that God is already going to give ideas that's going to be straight from the throne of God. Many people won't accept it because they've been scammed too far. They've been ripped off by the phony, by the wrong, about selling a certain product and you'll be rich. You can work from your home.

In America, that's what you want. We want to make money by doing nothing. It sounds wonderful, doesn't it? It's easy. Now, what it's meant to be? Easy. We are so attracted to that word. We're a microwave community. Of course, we like the 30-second job. We enjoy that and people are being scammed so much to where all you have to do is sit at home and type on this blog, and you'll make hundreds of dollars a day. People take that.

Every pop up around your e-mail isn't 100% real. I've had the same girl for the last many years. This type of thing is still popping up on the side of my e-mail saying, "I want to meet you." She has an aged a bit. I mean it's the same picture. They ought to update it at least. If you're going to have a scam out there, you got to at least have a good one. It's very annoying.

Jim and Lori Bakker

Now, understand I'm going to get at some nitty-gritty. You're ready for some nitty-gritty? I haven't started with this stuff yet. That was just the icing. Now, we're getting down to the cake. There are some people that fell into some illegal acts that did some things that were not of God, went to prison and God forgave them. God redeemed them but now they're doing what they did to get into prison the first time, and that is Jim Bakker and Lori Bakker.

I want you to understand God has been pushing on me to talk about them for a long time, and I just have bucked against it, not wanting to do it.

Here's the thing I'm saying. They're manipulating about selling money into a program. They're selling food and sowing fear in America is part of it. Selling a $30 bracelet that's supposed to be twine, they're supposed to be able to pick up anything or whatever. I'm telling you. It's almost so exaggerated that it's scary.

God said Lori Bakker is actually just as bad as Jim, and her house, some kind of Lori's house or something, I don't know all the facts. I know mostly by the spirit. There are some things that's going on there that are about to be exposed. There are taxes and they're doing a lot of illegal things where money is concerned. They're not reporting their salaries. The FBI is already watching them. They just want to build up a big enough case at this time. We won't see Jim again unless he repents.

Let me go ahead and say this. I'm not saying this to put down a man. I'm saying this because if anything, he needs to repent. He needs to begin to realize that maybe he doesn't need to be on television, because I think it pulls him into that arena. When he got out of prison, he was a changed man. He was an anointed man and he became a mighty man, but somewhere along the line, he picked up some things. This is the why I'm saying these things because he's manipulating. Many people are sowing millions of dollars into that ministry and they're doing it because of fear of being sold every week.

I used to be a pastor of a church and many people would buy barrels and barrels of food just in case something happened. You know what? God is raising up a church that's supposed to be like the days of Moses. Now, we're supposed to not be looking at the natural for food. You know what? I would rather die than have a barrel of food behind me if I can't believe in the supernatural, the God that I serve. Our trust should be in God, not in a barrel of food. There's nothing wrong with having some extra food when we know winter is coming or something is coming about that.

Let me go ahead and say. Some people are stockpiling so much that you know what's going to happen, is they're going to be the only ones with food if we did have a disaster. You know what? That opens a door for looters. If anything, they're putting targets on them, and I know some people that are actually buying filters to filter their urine so they can drink it. I don't know about you but I'd rather go to heaven. I'd rather be a martyr for God than to filter out any of my urine.

This got to be bad stuff. The fear that's being sold. The fear is being sold every week, and it's so deep in people's lives that they're fearing about every little thing. People were trembling over 9/11. I know some prophetic people that were prophesying there was going to be another natural disaster, a big disaster, the terrorist attack, 9/11. I wrote in an envelope and sealed it before 9/11 this year came that said nothing is going to happen. You say why because I wanted that prophetic word to be sealed so nobody can see it. You guess what? Nothing happened.

I'm telling you. The reason why is because all this fear that's being sold, let go ahead and say something. There will be more terrorist attacks. There will be more natural disasters. There will be an end of the world, but who are you going to be seeking? Are you going to be looking for your barrel pot? Are you going to be looking for your filter for your urine? What are you going to do? I'm looking to God. I want to believe that if He wants to bring release of manna from heaven for me to step into the next arena of life, then He will. If something happens and I don't get it, then praise God. I have fought the good fight of faith. I have finished my race. I have finished my course.

The Harbinger

Now, understand this is what God directed me to. There's a book called The Harbinger. Some of you have heard it. He's a very popular rabbi, but he's very associated with Jim Bakker. He talks about the end times and then Jim Baker sells the food. You understand what I just said there? He has some truth in his books. He has some truth in his teachings, but he has a lot of things that he is missing. He was one that prophesied about 9/11 being another disaster taking place this year. I just watched the video about 9/13 or 14 about what was supposed to happen in 9/11.

I love to watch that. Jesus was supposed to return last year too, but that's beside the point. I'm telling you there's things being prophesied. The Harbinger actually means a sign like a sign of judgment. He refers to the 9/11 as a sign of judgment upon America, and I do agree that America was supposed to have some things happen that was allowed by God. The thing is what he is preaching is sowing fear. You can get so caught up on the end times if you don't step out of it. Guess what? You forget about the now time. God is never going to have revival with some of these people because they're always looking to the end.

Well, if you read my Bible which should be your Bible, God is coming back for a glorious church without spot or without wrinkle. He's going to rise up in the last days as mighty men and women of God walking across the Earth. That hasn't happened yet.

Covertness False Prophets

There's ministers and I mean that, I really do. Again, I'm not apologizing because they invited me to see a minister. This minister looked at me like I was the only person in the room that shouldn't be there. That night, he began to tell people that miracles were going to happen that night according to the offering they gave. He opened a guitar case and opened it up right in front of the whole sanctuary, and he said, "I want you to bring your jewelry and your money, and throw it in the guitar case and whatever you put in here is the amount of miracles you're going to get. If you don't put your jewelry in here, you won't get your miracle."

Everybody started throwing their wedding rings in, all kinds of jewelry and watches. I didn't move just so you know. Then he started doing guess prophecy. Somebody is hurting in their back and he looked around trying to see if anybody responded. Since they didn't he kept looking closer. This was a show. Then after praying for a couple of people where nothing happened, he began to say. Tomorrow night, there's going to be more miracles. Well, guess what? There was none the first night. It's a fraud.

I'm telling you. This was a man of God. I met him many years ago and he had a right spirit, but somewhere along the line he picked up a covetousness spirit. Covetousness is one of the signs of a false prophet. You can find that in the Defeating the Demonic Realm book. Covetousness is one of the signs of a false prophet, and that's what he is doing. I'm telling you. We need to think about that. He is saying you are going to pay for your miracle. The bible doesn't indicate that.

If anything, Jesus did miracles for the poor. They asked for offering. Here is the Scripture that they are manipulating to bring true. It's the Scripture and this is not one man. This is many men and women of God across the earth that is doing it, but the scripture they're using is they laid all the offerings at the Apostle's feet. They sold their homes and laid the offerings at the Apostle's feet in the Book of Acts. It talks about that.

Let me go ahead and say. The Scripture says they did without being coerced. They never were asked to. They just did it because God laid it up on their heart to do it. I've had people throw hundred dollar bills on the stage as I'm preaching. I've had people give me their watch. They're really nice watch. They throw those things onto the stage because they were led by the spirit and God did something in their life because they were led. I am not going to stand in front of everybody and say you have to do this to get this. That's not what my God does and that's not what your God does either because He should be the same God.

Let's go another step further. If you haven't got upset yet, we're about to get there.

Chapter 4
False Teachings

I want to start out with a prophetic declaration. You're best life now. I will not lose sleep tonight worried about your best life now. I will not pray tonight for tomorrow worried about their best life now or whether they have self-esteem or their checkbook is balanced or they've got days of purpose in their life.

I will not lose sleep because one day every one of you will stand before God naked and be judged and some of you will be cast into hell. These are people dying. The wrath of God lays waste to your community. Even as we speak, how many people will be swept away even today by the wrath of God through death in hell?

You're worried about whether or not someone feels good about themselves? It's not about big ministry. There are some men here, and I could call them by name, have big ministries and they're going to die and go to hell. It is not about health. God is the judgment.

Here, I'm upset about the prosperity gospel, because of one of the big churches, 10,000 members, with the pastor having a couple of, you know, a jet and two big condos worth 3 million dollars in Florida and real estate everywhere, all over the place, and gets breaks from his church, so he's in trouble with the IRS.

I believe that the reward there is Christ, God ultimately. I believe in degrees of rewards in heaven, but ultimately, every reward is leading to God and he is the final reward. Because we have an all satisfying, glorious, final, high treasure called Jesus Christ or the father in heaven, we can rejoice in the midst of persecution.

Rejoice and be glad in that day. Great is your reward in heaven for so they persecuted the prophets. You're the salt of the earth. Now, what do you think the salt, if you just let it flow, let it flow? I'll tell you what it's not. Wealth. Here's why. Prosperity gospel is no gospel because what it does is offer to people what they want as natural people.

You don't have to be born again to want to be wealthy. Therefore, you don't have to be converted to be saved by the prosperity gospel. When you appeal to people to come to Christ on the basis of what they already want, first Corinthians 2 makes no sense. The natural man does not receive the things of the spirit. They are foolishness to him.

Therefore, if you offer to people what they do not consider foolishness in the natural man, you're not preaching the gospel. The prosperity gospel offers to people what they desperately want as fallen people, gives it to them and grows huge churches, and we export it to Africa and the Philippines, flying in with our jets, bilking of their money, and going back to our condos worth 3 million dollars.

It is horrific what we export as Americans. I can't believe what we tolerate in the church. I'm on a crusade to crucify the prosperity gospel. I hate the prosperity gospel because I love the glory of God.

Now he says, he says something unusual about them. He says that they are like wolves. That God is their belly. That God is their belly, but they look like sheep. Now, how is that? How is it that they look like sheep? By their flattering, smooth speech, that in an age of tolerance makes you think that they are the men most full of love.

They will never contradict. They will never create a scandal. They will never be offensive. They will never speak for things to anger men, but they have the smooth tongue of a serpent. They flatter men, and they give carnal men exactly what they want.

Now, let me tell you something about false teachers. You think so many times that people fall prey to false teachers, and that, in a sense, can be true at times. But I think the dominant thing in scripture is just the opposite. False teachers are God's judgment on people who don't want God, but in the name of religion plan on getting everything their carnal heart desires.

Joel and Victoria Osteen

That's why a Joel Osteen is raised up. Those people who sit under him are not victims of him. He is the judgment of God upon them because they want exactly what he wants, and it's not God. You can line them all up along with him. That's where it is because let's go over it. Let's just look for a minute at second Timothy, just quickly.

Chapter 4, verse 1. I solemnly charge you in the presence of God and of Christ Jesus who is to judge the living and the dead and by his appearing and his kingdom. Preach the word. Now, when he says preach the word, what is he saying? He follows it up with: Be ready in season and out of season to reprove, rebuke, exhort. Notice that that is not what these preachers do.

As a matter of fact, they boast in the fact that they do not reprove. They do not rebuke. It's not their ministry, and why do they say it's not their ministry? They have the ministry of love, they say. Well, then are you saying Christ didn't have a ministry of love because he reproved and rebuked and exhorted and so did Paul?

But now look, verse 3. For time will come, this shows you that men are not so much victims of false prophets, as false prophets are the judgment of God upon men who don't want God. For the time will come when they will not endure sound doctrine. Who are the people, the religious people, identified with Christianity? They will not endure sound doctrine.

They can't endure it. They hate it, or it bores them to tears. What do they do? But wanting to have their ears tickled, they will accumulate for themselves teachers. Everybody is this world, I hope you know this. Everyone in the world that's involved in Christianity knows that America is the birthplace of every heretical teaching on the face of the earth of ours.

Joel Osteen is now the largest, quote, unquote, church, I'm using the word loosely, in America, down in Houston.

You need to understand that he is a pagan religion in every sense. He's a quasi pantheist. Jesus is a footnote that satisfies his critics and deceives his followers.

The idea of his whole thing is that men have the power in themselves to change their lives. In his definitive book, Your Best Life Now, he says, and that ought to be a dead give away, since the only way this could be your best life is if you're going to hell. He says that anyone can create by faith and words the dreams he desires. Health. Wealth. Happiness. Success.

The list is always the same. Here's some quotes from his book, Your Best Life Now. If you develop an image of success, health, abundance, joy, peace, happiness, nothing on earth will be able to hold those things from you, end quote. See, that's the law of attraction that's a part of this kind of system. Here's another quote. All of us are born for earthly greatness. You were born to win. Win what?

God wants you to live in abundance. You were born to be a champion. He wants to give you the desires of your heart. Before we were formed, he prepared us to live abundant lives, to be happy, healthy, and whole. But when our thinking becomes contaminated, it's no longer in line with God's word, end quote. By the way, God's word is not the bible. God's word is that word that comes to us mystically, spiritually, that tells us what we should want.

Here's another quote. Get your thinking positive and he will bring your desires to pass. He regards you as a strong courageous, successful person. You're on your way to a new level of glory. How do you get there? Believe, he says.

Visualize and speak out loud. Same exact approach. Words release your power. Words give life to your dreams.

You have to take that part of God which exists in you and create your own reality. What is the source of this? Where does this come from? Satan? This is satanic. This is satanic. This is not just off-center. This is satanic. Why do I say that? Because health, wealth, prosperity, the fulfillment of all your dreams and your desires, that's what Satan always offers. That's called temptation.

Based on the lust of the flesh, the lust of the eyes, and the pride of life. That's exactly what corrupt, fallen, unregenerate want. That's why works so well, right. You can go right into Satan's system, make everybody feel religious and turn up their desires, their temptations in to somehow honorable desires.

I mean, what did Satan say to Jesus? Have some satisfaction. Why are you hungry? You need to eat. You need to be healthy, whole. Why would you let yourself be unpopular? Dive off the temple corner. Everybody will be wowed. You'll be the winner. You'll be the champion. You'll be the messiah. They'll hail you. Oh, by the way, if you just look over the kingdoms of the world, I'll give those to you, too.

That's satanic. Why are these false teachers so successful at what they do? Because they're in cahoots with the devil. Why is Satan successful? Because his temptations, although they might appear noble on the outside, are in perfect court with all the fallen, corrupt, selfish, proud, evil desires of sinners. This is a false kind Christianity, and false view of God.

I think preachers like this who preach this stuff hate the true God. I really agree with that. I believe they hate the true God, and they're afraid to death that somebody might find out who he really is.

My mom is a big fan of the Osteen's. I was a big fan of father Osteen. I am a big of fan of anybody who can have a lot of salvation, but guess what? If they're not going to keep it because of what's being preached it, then it's not salvation to me.

In her message, Victoria Osteen tells a massive congregation to realize that their devotion to God is not really about God, but it's about themselves. This just happened. Your devotion to God is about you. Forget God. Well, hallelujah. Well, if that's the case, then I'm going to go buy a box of Twinkies and that's going to be a devotion to myself, because it's all about me. Forget God. Why do I worship? Why do I read the word then if it's about me? It's really foolish, and I try to give grace. I give more grace than I should because here's the next thing that comes out of her mouth.

"I want you to know this morning. Just do good for your own self. Do good because God wants you to be happy. When you come to church when you worship him, you're not doing it for God. You're doing it for yourself because that's what makes God happy."

Let me go ahead and say. He inhabits the praises of His people. We all praise in Him. I have nothing to be praised for.

Joel Osteen tells Larry King, he says homosexuality is a sin, but I don't want to preach about it. You know why? Because he admitted to Oprah Winfrey that he has homosexuality in his church. He won't preach about it because he doesn't want to lose those members.

Larry King asked him, "What are your views on homosexuality?" to which Osteen replied, "The same that they've always been. I believe the scripture says that it is sin but I always follow that up by saying, you know what, we're not against anybody."

See, the Bible says that we're supposed to love everyone but just because somebody homosexual shows up into my service doesn't mean I've got to dance around that that's a sin. What he is doing is he's dancing. You know what? My grace would have been fine up to that point but then they go over the bandwagon.

Larry King pressed him. You know why? He's trying to get the facts out of him. You might not like Larry King but if you want to see whether a man of God is real or not, Larry King will find out. How can it be if we don't know what causes it? You don't know why you're heterosexual. There's a lot of things Larry ... Here's what he said, "I don't understand so I don't want to preach on it and preach about it."

> *You shall not lie with a male as with a woman. It is an abomination. (NKJ, Leviticus 18:22)*
>
> *If a man lies with a male as he lies with a woman, both of them have committed an abomination. They shall surely be put to death. Their blood shall be upon them. (NKJ, Leviticus 20:13)*

The bible clearly says that's an abomination for a man to live with a man, a woman live with a woman. King inquired, "Does gay marriage annoy you?" I'll tell you what, if I was sitting there, I would not have been politically correct, come on, I would have not looked good on camera and I would have gotten my Twitter blown up. Osteen said, "It doesn't annoy me. From a scripture point of view it's not what my faith would teach, but it doesn't annoy me."

The interview with Larry King is another example of a mixed message offered on homosexuality. He said, that if a homosexual believes in Christ is the next thing he said in a statement to Oprah Winfrey, "If a homosexual believes in Christ he could go to heaven with no need to repent because he believes."

Let me go ahead and say there's not an ashtray in heaven and there's not a gayby in heaven either. You know what a gayby is? It's when 2 homosexuals have baby. It's not a baby, it's a gayby. That's not meant to be funny. It's meant to be what it is. It's disgusting. Let's move on because I'm not done with this.

He was asked if Jesus was the only way to salvation to go to heaven. He replied that he believed that there was more than one way to get saved and to go to heaven. This was in a question comparing religions. A Muslim can find God, a Buddhist can find God, well, guess what, it's not the same God unless they say, "Jesus, come into my life. Forgive me of my sin." Jesus is said, "I am the way, the only way." Come on. It's the one way and any man of God that portrays himself as a man of God on television should be one to say Jesus is the only way. I don't care if my seats are filled with thousands of people or not.

They made the comment that they are after people, not after their sin. That is proven because their church is huge. They're after people not after sin. I guarantee you if you took Joel Osteen out of the pulpit and put me in that same pulpit that same church it would be a different church in about one week. I know we would lose thousands of members. They'd be like, "What? I'm in sin? No, I'm not. I haven't been in sin for all these years."

You know what? Nobody is going to go arm in arm with somebody preaching false doctrine. See Joel Osteen, I know that I know that I know, I know his heart was right before God when he took over that church when he began to minister it. His heart was always right but somewhere along the line he started to stop preaching the truth and started petting demons. He started allowing partial truths to be intermixed and here's one of the reasons why, Oprah Winfrey.

Oprah Winfrey

He's been on her show several times along with the next guy I'm going to talk about. Let me go ahead and say, I am led by the spirit of God and God told me many years ago that Oprah Winfrey has a heart that is already sold out to the demonic realm. She has said from her own mouth she doesn't really believe in God, but yet she has all godly things on her show that always is trying to push partial truths and push things away from God.

She was actually yelled at by somebody in her crowd one time whenever she said there was more than one way to God. The woman yelled from the crowd, "Jesus is the only way." She was like, "Yeah" she just shut her down. She had a religious panel on her show. I'm telling you, God, led me by the spirit and I'll tell you, I don't usually like to do this, but when God said type this certain thing, the first thing that pops up was this religion panel on her show.

What I mean by this these are several ministers, different types of ministers, priests and different things on her show to talk about homosexuality. The first minister, I hate to say minister, stated that he believed homosexuality is a gift from God. I'll tell you what. His white color should have turned black right then and there. I was so disgusted by that. I'm telling you what. Any man of God that says it's a gift from God should be shut up.

That is disgusting to even say that's a gift from God. Oprah big on saying there is more than one-way to God and she likes to refer to "or the light" whatever you believe in. Some people believe they're going to light when they die, "walk into the light." They're going to the wrong way, it's just the devil holding a flashlight saying, "Come here." You think I'm kidding, I meant what I just said.

Sin is sin and it separates us from God. Some sins will send us to hell unless we repent and this means to turn away from the lifestyle. Joel Osteen literally said from his own mouth, "I know we have several gay people in our church, but we welcome them and we love them." Well, guess what, I welcome any homosexual that come to my service, but guess what, by the end they will know it's sin. Then they have to make a choice. Repent or find the next church that accepts you.

By this point I was like, "God, I don't know what I'm saying here. Am I supposed to continue?" He said look at John 7:24, "Judge not according to the appearance but judge righteous judgment." 'We are supposed to judge. God sent us as judges in this earth. The mirror of God. God said many months ago, that he was about to raise prophets that were going to preach the truth and not deny the truth but preach it and stand on the word of God and let the world know the truth. I'm telling you what, I believe that there is truth need to be released.

Joseph Prince

This next person I need to mention, I was in a hotel room many miles from here, just ministered many hours and I was lying unconscious on my bed with the TV on. The certain gentleman by the name of Joseph Prince was preaching. I'm lying on my bed and then all of a sudden God said, "Rise up." I rose up in my bed just like I came out of a coffin because that's what I felt like. I was so tired. I looked at the screen and he said, "When you have been said and ask Jesus into your heart you're forgiven for every sin you will ever sin. You will never have to repent again."

I'm telling you what, I just had a Holy Ghost shut down. I was still messed up from the service and that just pulled me out into the natural. I wanted to jump on that TV and preach the truth. Here's some things I found out because God put this thing on my heart for a long time but millions, millions are at risk of spending eternity in hell because of what this man is preaching. You say "Why?" We should desire to talk about unity just as he preaches, our common salvation, but I don't believe we can do the way he does it.

He preaches a false grace. He preaches a grace over grace. He even puts in a book, I'm going to give many quotes from his book. It sold millions of copies. I was asked to be part of the distribution of this book and I said, "No way." I've been asked this book from our book company several times. They're like, "Oh, it's hot." I said, "No, it's not."

Here's the thing. Here's a short summary of many deadly heresies that are associated with Joseph Prince Destined to Reign. What I know is by the spirit and then God had me find all this text out of his own book, out of his own writing.

He says, "Asking forgiveness for sin is unnecessary for believers." Hallelujah. You know why? Because you believe, you don't have to ask for forgiveness. Well, isn't that wonderful? We can all just have about 12 beers tonight and we don't have to ask for forgiveness, hallelujah. Add a joint to the mix of it and go have some fornication and then we come back to church and say, "Hallelujah." I'm serious. This is coming from a man of God to thousands of congregations. I believe he has 17,000 minimum in his congregation. That's a church.

I was going to say I don't know what I'd do with that but I don't think I'll ever have that. I know God is going to give this a crowd in the days ahead, the reason why is because there are truth lovers out there that are going to come out of the woodwork that are going to finally realize these false teachings are driving them astray.

Another quote in his book is about Moses and Jesus taught opposite doctrines. Let me go ahead and say Moses really taught about Jesus coming. Jesus talked about Moses been. That's the only difference, I mean it's really a terrible thing. The next thing was, "The law brings condemnation and therefore Jesus removed it. Jesus removed the law."

Let me go ahead and say this. He removed the law of sin and death but the 10 commandments stayed in place. In other words we don't have to be subject to the law or bound to it. It doesn't mean we discard it. Sin is still sin. You know why this is so popular? Because it's easy Christianity. Come on. There's some religions that do that today.

Another thing was preaching the law makes people sin more. Therefore it should not be taught at church because it will harm your church congregation. In other words, we should just leave them ignorant. Don't preach the truth.

The bible says, "Preach the truth in love." Come on. Whether you know it or not. I am preaching pretty lovely about all this. About as lovely as I can preach about it I'm preaching it. The gift of righteousness is another one means we are righteous even if we are not. That's a gift. It's a gift of righteousness so in other words you're righteous no matter what.

Sounds pretty ignorant doesn't it? I can write a whole chapter just from the things I pulled and I skipped about 50 of them. They were just too obvious. I like something that's a little more complicated.

We have unconditional forgiveness. Let me go ahead and say this. That's a partial truth that is twisted. We do have unconditional forgiveness if we repent. He will forgive me. He has several times. Jesus forgives but we don't have unconditional. In other words we don't just get forgiven just because we did it.

God was perpetually angry in the Old Testament and perpetually happy in the New Testament. That's another quote that he had. In other words he was very happy in the New Testament that's why it was different. He was an angry God in the Old Testament.

If he was really an angry God in the Old Testament He would have killed the Israelites long before they died. Come on. He would have brought the second flood if he didn't love. Hallelujah. I won't stay there long because I don't need to.

There's another comment, "God does not judge nations for wickedness." He doesn't? Israel hasn't been punished because of their wickedness? God loves Israel and he's going to raise them up but there's judgment being released on them. We are experiencing judgment because we're not lifting up Israel. Come on. According to him there's none of that.

"If God judges people, cities and nations today then he should apologize to Jesus for the cross." I know that one confused me when I looked at it. I had to read about 4 times. It literally says, "If God judges people, cities and nations today then he should apologize to Jesus for the cross." In other words he's saying since Jesus died and rose again judgment is done. Then why was Paul so busy preaching about repentance? I'll get to Paul in a minute because he comments about that too.

He just pulls all the Bible out. That's what he does. That's like a shredder man. Again, this is a man of God that can preach. He can preach, man. He has a big crowd and he could use that to change a nation, but instead he's using it for personal gain.

"Believers are punished for sin." I guess believers go to a good hell. "We truly never stop sinning but God is okay with that." God says that the fivefold ministry is for the perfection or the saints. We might not be perfect but we are supposed to be coming into perfection. The bible says that we are all become new. In other words we're still becoming new. This just puts a stop to it. You just give up, I'm done.

There's another comment. This was terrible, wasn't it? It's a good book. A good book for killing. "We are not held more accountable to God when we know more nor do we face greater punishment if we fail having known the truth nor will we go through greater trials or tribulations as we draw close to God." The more you receive the more is required of you is what my bible says. In other words the more truth I know the more is going to be required to me.

What I did 20 years ago, I could do sin man, and still raise my hands to heaven but if I did it today, ooh, I'd be in trouble. God has a bigger stick for me today than he used to have. Some of you need to realize.

Another one, "The word of God doesn't produce faith only the word of Christ." In other words he's saying only what Jesus spoke produces faith. The bible he just threw out with that quote.

It's subtleties like this, like I said, I give grace for about first 10 of these and then I start stepping over like, "Now, you're just preaching false truth and you're actually preaching the false grace that's going to cause a lot of people to think they're going to go to heaven when they die and they're going to find their place in hell."

The next one, "The word of God and the word of Christ don't agree on some things." In other words everything Christ spoke sometimes doesn't line up with the bible. No, that is not even fact. The thing is, man, I'll tell you, this guy showed up on TBN and they cheered for him like he was the heavyweight champion of the world.

The next one said, "Christians cannot commit the unpardonable sin." Christians cannot commit the unpardonable sin. Yeah, because as soon as you commit it you're not a Christian anymore. That's the only way I could tell that to be a fact. But see, the way he believes you don't fall from Christianity once you've got it.

I don't know about you, but I really lost my salvation once. I mean I didn't just sin, I sinned hardcore. Come on. According to him, I never lost it. Technically, what he preaches is once saved always saved. That's a life for the pit of hell.

The next one, I'm trying to get through these, "Part of Jesus' teaching is not applicable because it's Old Testament." Part of what Jesus said was preaching about Old Testament so it doesn't apply today. See this? This stuff don't look too bad when you surround it with a bunch of flowers but when you pull the thorn out it looks bad, don't it? This one makes you second look at it and then you pull it out and it's like, well, this one looks bad.

We can't take doctrine from the gospels because Jesus had not risen from the dead yet. The bible says we're supposed to preach the gospel. What are we supposed to preach if we can't take it? I know you're all scratching your chin, your hair, your head.

This one messed me up a little bit. "Paul's the lead authority on doctrine, not Jesus, because he addressed the church." Paul probably was the most powerful man next to Jesus Christ as a man in the word of God, but nobody on this earth, has ever been on this earth is as mighty man as Jesus is.

"Confession of sins for believers is about being open with God, not about repentance because we're already forgiven."

In other words you're just open. That's like coming home after you've committed adultery and saying, "Hey, honey, I just had sex with another woman. What's for dinner?" You're just open about it. There's no repentance. Come on. I hope somebody is getting my point.

Confession of sins ... Listen, the next one, "Even though the Book of John was written to the church, the opening chapters only for the agnostics. Therefore we can disregard the instructions to confess our sins." I can stand on my head, punch myself in it about 5 times and still not seeing that.

I can't find this truth. There's a reason why began to preach this. He had a transformation that was from the pit of hell and he went for it. Listen, the next one, "Confession of sin is unnecessary because we would have to confess all the time." Really? It would be a lot easier for us to receive that. Well, God's not going to have us repent because we're going to have to do it all the time.

Let's go to this one. "Not only should we not teach the law from the pulpit, we should only teach grace" even though the New Testament gives a ... This is my part, 1050 commands for believers to obey but we're supposed to skip that part. Over 1050 times in the bible we're supposed to obey His command but according ... I'm talking about God's command, we're not supposed to teach the law, we only should teach grace.

The Bible has got a bunch of stuff that's not supposed to be in it. The Holy Spirit does not convict us of sin or judgment. You know why? Because it's not holy what you've got. If you have a spirit that's not convicting you of your sin then it's not holy. It's a demon.

Another one "Satan loves the 10 commandments." After reading all these others I believe the only reason that's in there that he says Satan loves the 10 commandments is because the 10 commandments keep us under bondage of the law. No, it keeps us from going to hell.

If we throw out the 10 commandments I can murder somebody and still go to heaven. Is that right? Is that right at any of your churches? We go to a lot of different churches but I don't think any of us we go to our church and say, "I just shot somebody. Hallelujah."

"We shouldn't talk about sin, repentance or judgment from the pulpit, we should only talk about the goodness of God." I'm about done. I've only got about 10 more of these. I've got about one chapter of the book out of it. Just in my stuff.

"Abraham had a covenant of grace but Moses had an inferior covenant of works." In other words ... There's one comment in there, I'm not going to say it exactly correct because I didn't write it down, but something about the only reason the 10 commandments was given to Moses because he was angry. More or less he's trying to say that Moses helped out with the 10 commandments because he was angry.

I know he had a messed up church but my goodness that's a lot to bloody your hands for. This sounds pretty messed up don't it? I don't know about you, but how does a church get filled every week for this?

The next one, "Repentance doesn't involve mourning or sorrow or confession for sin, it just means you changed your mind." In other words somebody can go, "I changed my mind." I hope some of you just got how serious that looked. That wasn't a cigarette. I just changed my mind. I hope somebody is getting this.

The next one, "The doctrine of repentance from sin is not for believers. Grace is a teacher so we don't need the law." He actually referred to on one show "mother grace." Mother grace, it sounds like he almost went Catholic.

"Falling from grace doesn't mean sinning it means reverted to the law. If you don't teach the law you are a man pleaser." I don't know what that meant. "Fasting in unnecessary and is only in the New Testament because fasting enthusiasts added it later."

I know some Bibles have changed over the years but gee whiz. "When Satan tempted Jesus to turn the stones to bread he was actually tempting Jesus to get nourishment from the law instead of trusting in the love of God." We can go on and on. Here's the final quote that I found in their source of why he wrote the book and has preached this false teaching for many years. "The Lord told me many years ago, son, your ministry is to roll away the stone."

Let me explain to you what this means. In the story of Jesus resurrected commanded the people to roll away the stone from Jesus' tomb, my friend, the stone is a picture of the law. He's literally said with his own quote, he had to stop preaching the law because God told him to. From that day forward he never ever preached against sin and he preached about once saved always saved, grace, grace, grace, too much grace.

I would suggest that you or any ministry personally devoted to the concept of rejecting the laws of God and the name of God is in fact promoting lawlessness and rebellion in authority which is why a common symptom of these heretics' teachings is church splits, license, immorality, rogue ministers who refuses correction and accountability to qualified spiritual leaders.

I understand this is a time of change and there are preachers that are preaching like they had never preached before but this is not truth. This is false. I understand times have changed but understand I disagree to where I'm going to preach something that's going to satisfy my church every week. If I find out you like it this way, or like it that way, I'm not going to preach it.

Well, guess what? That's a lie from the pit of hell. I would rather have a hundred kind of crowd every night and preach the truth and tell what God says than to ever dance around anything and try to give you some kind of grace message that is straight from the pit of hell and that you could die in a week or month or a year or 10 years from now, or 100 years from now and you are going to go to hell because you received what I preached.

Well, let me go ahead and say. I would rather you be there on judgment day and somebody look you square in the eye and say, "Bill Vincent told you the truth and you denied or received it." I would rather that than anything else. That's what angers me. It's not me coming against any man or any ministry or even Oprah Winfrey. It's coming against what's being spoken out of their mouths to corrupt our nation and make them receive homosexuality as normal, to receive what's going on in our nation is normal.

Currently there are many homosexual ministries and churches rising up because of these mega preachers teachings. We need more Christians to take a stand and preach the truth.

About the Author

Bill Vincent is an Apostle and Author with Revival Waves of Glory Ministries in Litchfield, IL. Bill and his wife Tabitha work closely in every day ministry duties. Bill and Tabitha lead a team providing Apostolic over sight in all aspects of ministry, including service, personal ministry and Godly character.

Bill is a believer in Jesus Christ in the fullness of power with signs and wonders. Bill has an accurate prophetic gift, a powerful revelatory preaching anointing with miracles signs and wonders following.

Bill Vincent is no stranger to understanding the power of God, having spent over twenty years as a Minister with a strong prophetic anointing, which taught him the importance of deliverance by the power of God. Bill has more than thirty prophetic books available all over the world. Prior to starting his ministry, Revival Waves of Glory he spent the last few years as a Pastor of a Church and a traveling prophetic ministry.

Bill Vincent helps the Body of Christ to get closer to God while overcoming the enemy. Bill offers a wide range of writings and teachings from deliverance, to the presence of God and Apostolic cutting edge Church structure. Drawing on the power of the Holy Spirit through years of experience in Revival, Spiritual Sensitivity and deliverance ministry, Bill now focuses mainly on pursuing the Presence of God and breaking the power of the devil off of people's lives.

His book Defeating the Demonic Realm was published in 2011 and has since helped many people to overcome the spirits and curses of satan. Since then Bill's books have flooded the market with his writings released just like he prophesies the Word of the Lord.

Bill Vincent is a unique man of God whom has discovered; powerful ways to pursue God's presence, releasing revelations of the demonic realm and prophetic anointing through everything he does. Bill is always moving forward at a rapid pace and there is sure to be much more released by him in upcoming years.

Recommended Books

By Bill Vincent
Overcoming Obstacles
Glory: Pursuing God's Presence
Defeating the Demonic Realm
Increasing Your Prophetic Gift
Increase Your Anointing
Keys to Receiving Your Miracle
The Supernatural Realm
Waves of Revival
Increase of Revelation and Restoration
The Resurrection Power of God
Discerning Your Call of God
Apostolic Breakthrough
Glory: Increasing God's Presence
Love is Waiting – Don't Let Love Pass You By
The Healing Power of God
Glory: Expanding God's Presence
Receiving Personal Prophecy
Signs and Wonders
Signs and Wonders Revelations
Children Stories
The Rapture
The Secret Place of God's Power
Building a Prototype Church
Breakthrough of Spiritual Strongholds
Glory: Revival Presence of God
Overcoming the Power of Lust

Glory: Kingdom Presence of God
Transitioning to the Prototype Church
The Stronghold of Jezebel
Healing After Divorce
A Closer Relationship With God
Cover Up and Save Yourself
Desperate for God's Presence
The War for Spiritual Battles
Spiritual Leadership
Global Warning
Millions of Churches
Destroying the Jezebel Spirit
Awakening of Miracles
Deception and Consequences Revealed
Are You a Follower of Christ
Don't Let the Enemy Steal from You!
A Godly Shaking
The Unsearchable Riches of Christ
Heaven's Court System
Satan's Open Doors
Armed for Battle
The Wrestler
Spiritual Warfare: Complete Collection
Growing In the Prophetic
The Prototype Church: Complete Edition
Faith
The Angry Fighter's Story
Understanding Heaven's Court System

Web Site:
www.revivalwavesofgloryministries.com

www.ingramcontent.com/pod-product-compliance
Lightning Source LLC
Chambersburg PA
CBHW072112290426
44110CB00014B/1896